JOHN IKE | 9 HOUSES, 9 STORIES

INTERVIEWS BY MITCHELL OWENS

PRINCIPAL PHOTOGRAPHY BY RICHARD POWERS WITH ANITA SARSIDI

VENDOME

NEW YORK · LONDON

CONTENTS

13   INTRODUCTION

17   RANCH HOUSE, CALIFORNIA | OWNER AND TYLER VELTEN

55   SEASIDE VILLA, NEW JERSEY | MIA JUNG

119 ODDFELLOWS HALL, MAINE | ROBERT A. BAIRD

137 MODERN SHINGLISH, NEW YORK | ROSS R. PADLUCK AND ANITA SARSIDI

167 MOUNTAIN LODGE, CALIFORNIA | JOEL BARKLEY

199 CONTEMPORARY CRAFTSMAN, NEW YORK | FRANK DEBONO

227 GLASS HOUSE, WASHINGTON | TOM KLIGERMAN

249 VINEYARD ESTATE, CALIFORNIA | CARL BAKER

269 CASITA, CALIFORNIA | JUDY KAMEON

301 ACKNOWLEDGMENTS

302 CREDITS

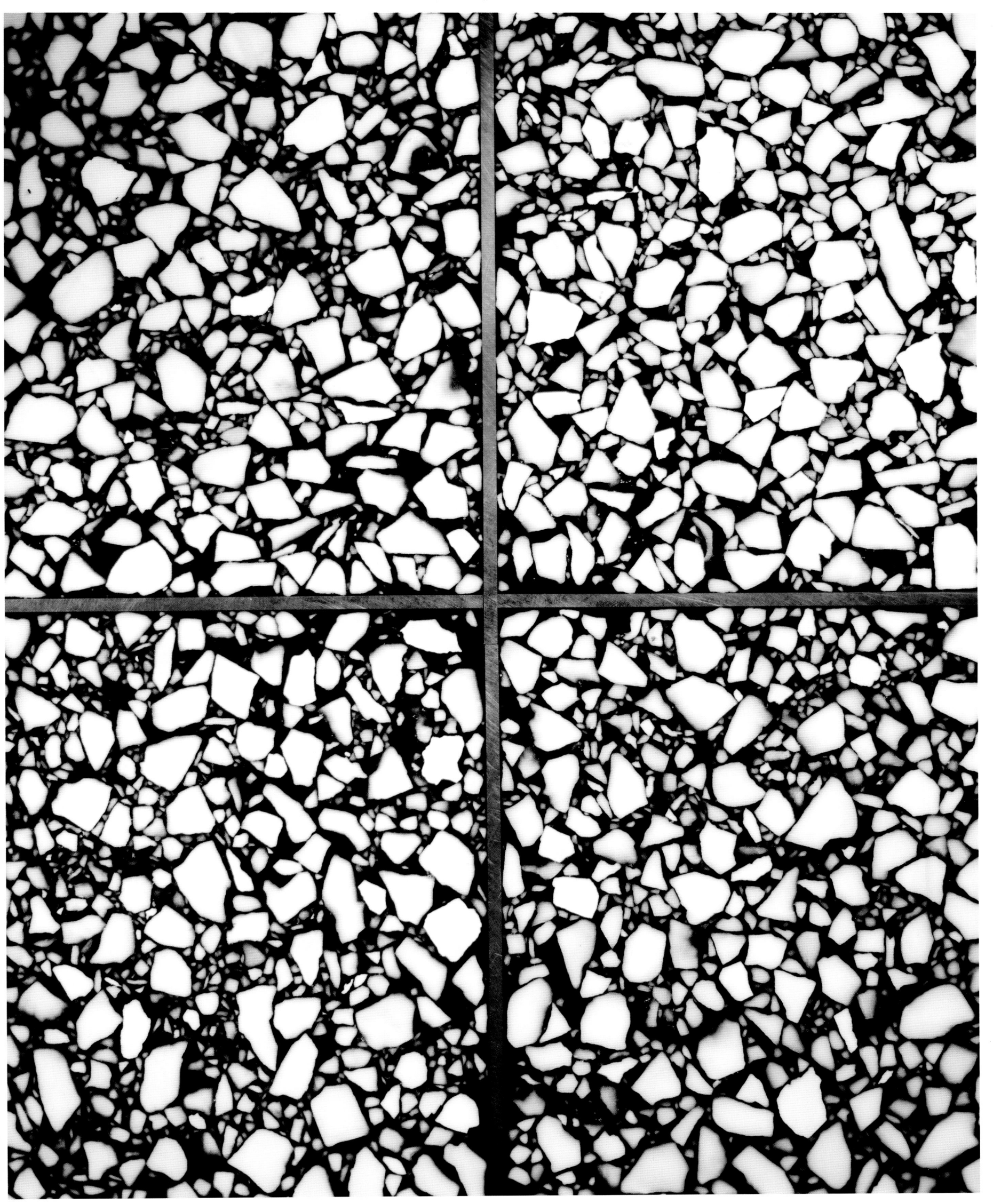

INTRODUCTION

For decades, Ike Kligerman Barkley has been a collaboration of three like-minded partners and friends. Thomas Kligerman (who joined me in 1989), Joel Barkley (who came on board in the 1990s), and I have shared a common sensibility and devotion to mining the annals of architectural history, often utilizing unbelievably disparate sources, and combining them with our clients' wishes to create unique, site-specific houses. Though our projects may have historical precedents underpinning everything from their silhouettes to their details, they are thoroughly modern conceptions that are technically advanced and are designed to facilitate our clients' lifestyles and address their needs.

The projects included in *9 Houses, 9 Stories* represent work that has been produced at IKB over the past several years. Some of the houses were designed in my studio; others, under the watchful eye of my partners. That being said, the attributions represent many shades of gray, because every IKB commission is influenced by more people than the architect alone. Scores of people and thousands of decisions go into the creation of these houses. Though a strong shared vision is an absolute, it is the relationships among the people involved in the creation and execution of the project that ultimately determine its success and the happiness of all.

With the help of our gifted writer, Mitchell Owens, *9 Houses, 9 Stories* teases out some of the subtleties of these relationships and more accurately describes how these individuals actually work with us— and how they manifest themselves in everything we produce, from a couple's getaway nestled in a forest in the Pacific Northwest to a multipurpose restored historic Oddfellows Hall in Maine. The conversations include the voices of clients, architects and designers on staff, consultants, builders, landscape designers, and craftspeople, and last but not least, the photographers and stylists who create the images of these private homes.

9 Houses, 9 Stories is intended as a salute to our work. It also marks the official end to the thirty-four-year run of Ike Kligerman Barkley, since we have now split into three successor firms: Kligerman Architecture & Design, Ike Baker Velten, and Joel Barkley's private architectural practice. In creating these houses, we found it most efficient and satisfying to develop them independently in our own studios while still relying on the input from one another, both to further our individual creativity and to utilize the various areas of expertise that we're fortunate to possess.

Over the years, several extremely capable protégés have taken on a greater role in our collective work, and at times they have become the primary authors of projects. So much so, in fact, that it often becomes difficult to ascertain where certain concepts and details come from. At Ike Baker Velten, based in Oakland, California, I am joined by architects Carl Baker and Tyler Velten, each of whom has been an important force at IKB's West Coast office. The three of us have often worked so closely that the same idea seems to spring forth simultaneously. Many of our references are similar, including an admiration for mid-century West Coast and Pacific Rim masters such as Cliff May, William Wurster, and Vladimir Ossipoff and for the styles and intricacies seen in the vernacular architecture of the greater Western United States. Tyler and Carl are also admiring of several contemporary international talents, among them Japan's Kengo Kuma and Teronobu Fujimori and Chile's Smiljan Radic.

Creative inspirations like those will serve as a springboard for us to explore new ideas, fresh approaches, and unique domestic statements, including one that Carl likes to call "wooly modernism," wherein the modernist fetish for clean lines is less important than a shaggy sense of warmth and well-being. "Our work seeks to find a balance between style, detail, and context," Tyler explains, "between that which is predictable and that which appears unpredictable." Ultimately, what matters at Ike Baker Velten is that every house is the best it can be, one where invention, curiosity, and provocation coalesce into a comforting whole.

JOHN IKE

So many people want master-of-the-universe views, but my husband and I chose this site for our house because it did not offer anything like that. It is not on top of a hill, all superior and looking down; it is on a hillside, which is not the easiest profile to work with. Another architecture firm might have wanted us to flatten the site or move the house elsewhere, but IKB was comfortable with the irregularities and embraced them. Tucking the house into the land gave us multiple views: all of them different, some of them sweeping, some of them intimate, and each of them great. Tyler Velten, a senior associate and co-design director in IKB's San Francisco office, called it the most beautiful site he has ever worked on. It is a classic California savannah, with giant oak trees and stands of redwood. We wanted the house to snuggle into the landscape, to really mesh with the light, the grasses, the trees, the scents.

The previous house that we built was Shingle Style, but this time around we did not come to the table with a specific style in mind. We knew what we did not want, though: no glass-and-steel box and no hacienda, but we were open to letting the house be somewhere in the middle. John kept sending us books about Cliff May, the master of the ranch house, even though I told him that I hate ranch houses. It was not until we saw the sketch that he literally scribbled on a cocktail napkin after our first meeting that I recognized how lovely the house he had in mind would be. It was spot on: a building that followed the slope of the hill and was filled with sunlight on all sides. You could call it a ranch house or maybe a California bungalow, but at the same time it is neither. John has described it as a cocktail, because it has mid-century elements inspired by May and William Wurster, Craftsman-like woodwork, some detailing that suggests a lodge in upstate New York, and lots of glass. I asked John, "What style of house is that?" And he said, "It's your style."

John and Tyler stretched our minds when it was necessary, yet they also listened carefully. We wanted an understated house, and though it might look large from a distance because of its massing, it is the perfect size: 4,100 square feet. I would not change the footprint in any way. My husband wanted everything on one level, because this was going to be our very last house. The structure follows the hill, though, so there is a lot of variation, with the living room at the bottom of the hill and the other rooms rising up the slope. When people walk in the front door, they just see trees, the Pacific Palisades, and then the horizon—I don't know how you figure that out as an architect, but it is breathtaking. We can see where the sun sets and the moon rises, and though I wanted an east-facing bedroom, John and Tyler shifted it so that the morning light rakes across the room instead of blinding our eyes as we wake up.

We really like good lighting, and since we cook a lot, we wanted the kitchen to have the right amount of illumination. John heard that and came up with an ingenious light fixture shaped like a racetrack and just built it—it was not something we had thought of or even really signed off on, but it is absolutely perfect and ingeniously addresses the lighting issues that concerned us. It is one of the best features in the house.

Trust was a consistent element in our relationship with IKB. We discussed ideas, my husband and I offered strong opinions, John pushed back in the gentlest way when he disagreed, and then he and Tyler proceeded to design the way they thought best, guiding us along through the entire process. Everyone in the firm is mild mannered but persistent. Even though the house took several years to develop and build and went through various iterations, we all kept circling back to that original concept: John's sketch on the cocktail napkin. That was what we fell in love with in the first place, and nothing we did could interfere with that.

The project was not especially easy, but what perfect house is? We were constantly scrutinizing details, finishes, cabinet designs, and materials, which were hugely important to us. The architecture had to defer to nature, so we literally brought to a meeting leaves from the site, stones, decomposed granite, even moss. My husband went out and took photographs of the building site from various viewpoints, and Tyler then tweaked the renderings to create a coherent palette. The materials are pretty uncomplicated: a Corten steel roof, natural-colored stucco, a little bit of stone, Port Orford cedar for the interior woodwork, windows made of Douglas fir and steel that has been painted to blend with the wood, and some concrete that had to be tinted just a bit more green to work. It is a house that knows its place, and every day we fall in love with it all over again.

44

Page 15: Detail of windowsill.

Pages 18–19: South elevation.

Page 21: Breakfast room.

Pages 22–23: Living room.

Page 24 left: Living room mantel.

Page 24 right: Detail of table.

Page 25: View from dining room into living room.

Page 26: Detail of transom.

Page 27: Dining room.

Page 28: View from dining room into living room.

Page 29: Details of settee in dining room.

Page 31: Stairs leading to dining room and entry.

Page 33: Kitchen.

Page 35: View into family room.

Pages 36–37: Back hall.

Pages 38–39: Bedroom.

Page 40: Bathroom.

Page 41: Detail of glass-brick shower.

Page 43: Dressing room.

Page 44: Site plan.

Page 45: Back porch.

Pages 46–47: North elevation.

Opposite: California live oak.

Overleaf: View of California Coastal Ranges.

SEASIDE VILLA, NEW JERSEY | MIA JUNG

Many interior designers struggle with architecture that isn't very good, on projects where the way the rooms are to be furnished is the second thought, never the first. As director of interiors at IKB, I'm lucky because I can get involved with a project from the beginning, as the house is being planned; from my perspective, those projects are especially successful. That early start allows me not only to do my job best but also to appreciate the quality of the architecture that surrounds what I do and to understand the world of difference between IKB and other firms. I get to collaborate with three very different architects, men with very different approaches. I've come to understand what each of them cares deeply about and, conversely, what each one is comfortable handing over to me. On the bright side, that means I've developed the ability to work with anybody. Not that it's the easiest job in the world at times. Some of the firm's projects can go on and on for years because that's how the client operates, so I try to meditate every day.

Being involved from the start of any house or apartment is preferable because I get to weigh in on the practical details, such as whether there is enough room to install curtain hardware or whether the floor registers are in the least disruptive place for placing furniture. I'll prepare a thorough checklist based on the architectural plans as they progress, and sometimes I find myself fulfilling the role of project editor. There's a lot of overlap in my role. For a residential commission on Martha's Vineyard, I remember being presented with a house-wide paneling program that was to be executed in thirteen different finishes. I diplomatically narrowed that down to six; thirteen was really too many.

One important thing I've learned over my twenty-three years at IKB is that John always has a very strong vision for his houses, inside and out, and he doesn't really alter the overall vision. By the time I became involved with this particular residence on a beautiful stretch of the Jersey shore, the architectural aspects had been designed, and the hard finishes had been selected. John was already sourcing furnishings at auctions for the clients, so I had to work with those choices, because he likes interiors and exteriors to be visually coherent, to relate to each other.

John's projects always have a story line, a narrative. I always stress to the clients that if they can give him the freedom to do his job—to trust him and let him go in that direction—then the project will end up amazing. He told the New Jersey couple that his concept was an old Italian villa that had been renovated in the 1970s, not unlike the villa in the Luca Guadagnino movie *Call Me by Your Name,* and they loved the idea. The exterior of the house is black stucco, as if it had been constructed from lava rock, and the interiors are white plaster and terrazzo; it's a house with a very strong sense of character and a simple palette that reminds John of historic buildings in Catania, a city on the eastern coast of Sicily. It also explains why he had already begun to source vintage Italian club chairs and some specific twentieth-century lighting. But the New Jersey house couldn't be entirely Italian, and it definitely could not be a period piece.

I suggested to John that we mix in some contemporary furnishings in styles and materials that would be sympathetic to the house in his imagination. It was a vision that had already been adjusted slightly anyway because John had thrown in a couple of curve-balls. He had taken a trip to Guadalajara and thought that maybe the New Jersey interiors could reflect a Latino-Mediterranean crossover, because some of the eighteenth- and nineteenth-century houses he had seen in Guadalajara reminded him of Sicilian houses of the same era, as did some of Mexico's mid- to late twentieth-century furnishings. So he made note of bedding, ceramics, and textiles that he thought would look well in the New Jersey house and resonate with the Italian designs he admired. I ended up liaising with Bibiana Huber and her team at Huber Design, whom John had discovered in Mexico, to locate ceramics and textiles, and I also tapped many of my own sources in the United States for similar items. I think it turned out to be a very interesting synthesis. John and I work well together—I know where he wants to go.

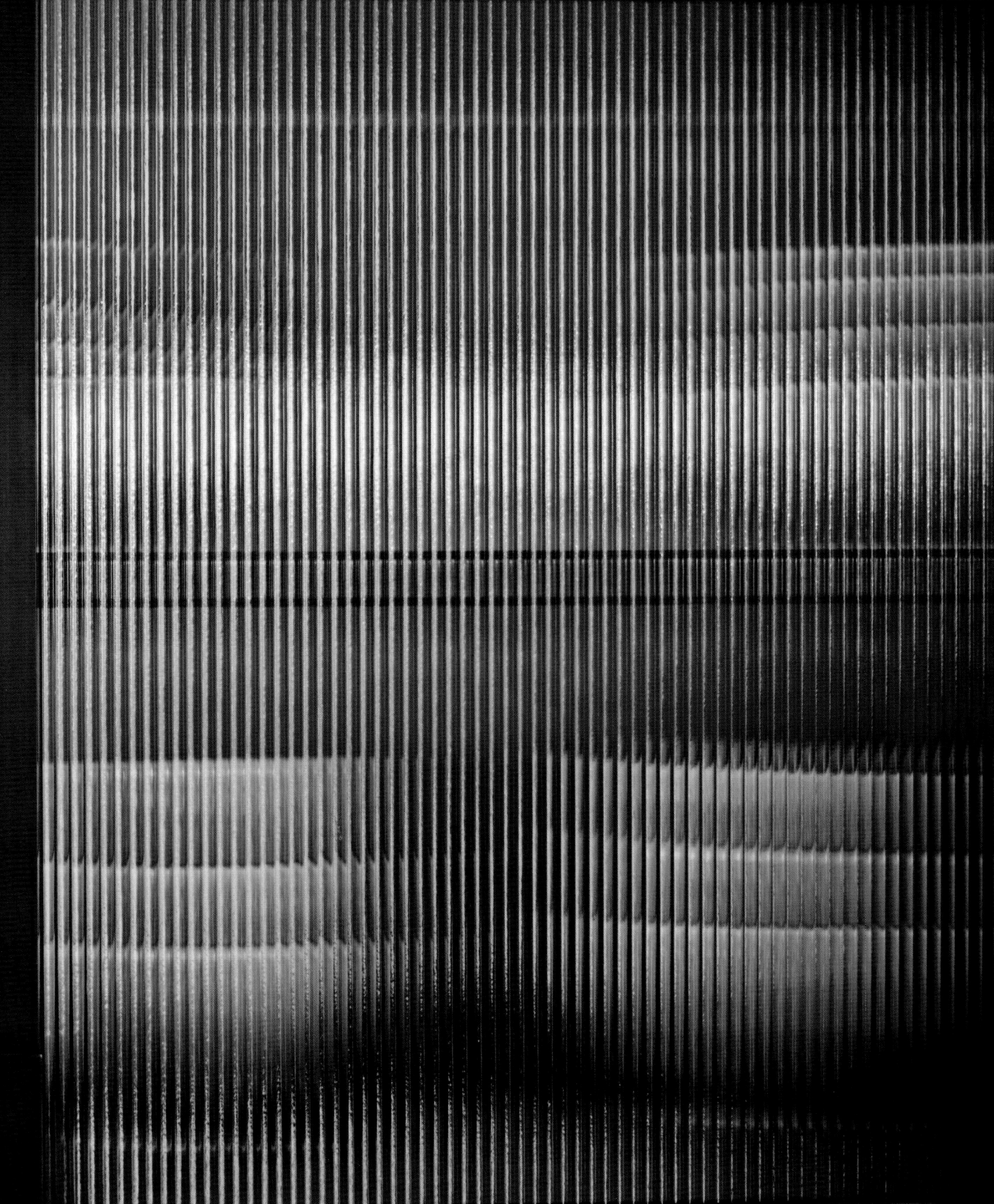

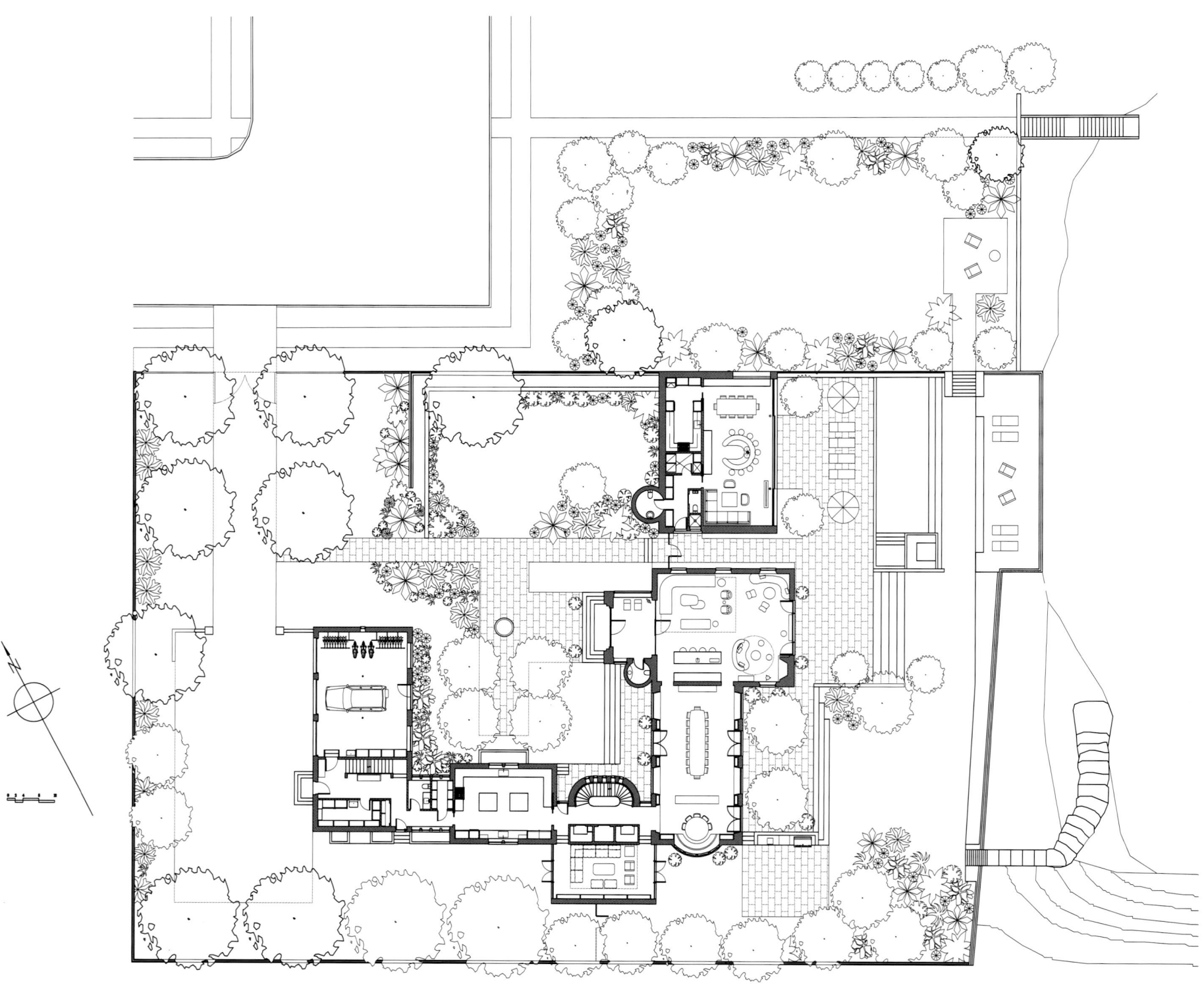

Page 53: Detail of living room coffee table.

Pages 56–57: View of the house from the northwest.

Page 59: Pendant in shadow.

Page 60: Front entrance.

Page 61: Pendant.

Pages 62–65: Living room.

Page 66: Ettore Sotsass totem.

Page 67: Mantel detail.

Pages 68–69: Living room.

Pages 70–71: Detail of table and rug.

Page 72: Bar.

Page 73: Detail of bar.

Pages 74–76: Dining room.

Page 77: Detail of dining room chair.

Page 79: Door to terrace.

Page 80: Rolling cabinet.

Page 81: Breakfast bay.

Page 83: Powder room.

Page 84: Detail of railing.

Pages 85, 87: Staircase.

Page 88: Detail of chandelier.

Page 89: Stair hall.

Page 90: Detail of shelves.

Page 91: Family room.

Pages 92–93: Detail of kitchen cabinet.

Page 94: Kitchen.

Page 95: Detail of kitchen hood.

Page 97: Back stair.

Pages 98–99: Bedroom.

Page 100: Detail of shelves.

Page 101: Bathroom.

Page 102: Detail of fireplace.

Page 103: Fireplace.

Page 104: Dressing room.

Page 105: Detail of bedroom.

Page 107: Detail of dressing room cabinet.

Page 108: Bathroom.

Page 109: Detail of bathroom.

Page 110: Site plan.

Page 111: Seaside elevation.

Opposite: Detail of balcony.

Overleaf: Terrace.

ODDFELLOWS HALL, MAINE | ROBERT A. BAIRD

John and I have worked together for years, ever since the 1980s, when he worked at Bob Stern's office in New York City. My father, Stephen T. Baird, was an architect who was summoned to Utah from Manhattan by the Mormon church to restore the Zion Mercantile Department Store in Salt Lake City. It had a cast-iron façade, and my father figured out how to repair it. Restoration was a field that I grew up with as a result, and my brothers and I ultimately founded Historic Arts & Casting in Salt Lake City, and Ike Kligerman Barkley is one of our longtime clients. We recently made light fixtures for a house that John designed for clients on the Jersey shore. He always says that if he makes a wish, we can make it come true.

We also have roots in Brooklin, Maine: I because of my love of wooden boats and my past working for the National Trust for Historic Pres- ervation; he because of a period of time spent attending Outward Bound. He hated the experience but loved the area and has always called it home. My wife and I now live in Brooklin full time. John and I were having lunch one day, and he said, "Somebody needs to restore the Oddfellows Hall." The Independent Order of Odd Fellows was a fraternal organization similar to the Masons, and the Italianate four-square building, built in 1896 and crowned by a mansard roof, was the biggest in Brooklin. Each of the floors is 2,600 square feet. The third floor was the lodge, the second floor had been a meeting place for the community, and the first floor was a small grocery store. Oddfellows Hall had fallen into a state of disrepair by the time we became aware of it, though I always thought it could be a great place to live and work, if only someone would take it on as a project. John agreed, and said, "Yeah, let's get some people to purchase it and restore the building."

The three people ended up being me, John, and Steve White, the owner of Brooklin Boatyard and grandson of *New Yorker* writer E. B. White, who penned some of his best stories here, including *Charlotte's Web*. We each decided to take a floor, and we all agreed that the properties had to be income producing. John and I chose to turn our floors into vacation rental units, and Steve moved his boat- yard into the street-level space. That's really how the whole project got started. John and his staff did all the drawings, and Steve lent financial support. First, we replaced the roof; then we focused on bringing the clapboard exterior of the building back to life, including the removal and restoration of all the original windows, replacing the glass with historically appropriate panes. After that, we took our attention indoors, upgrading the electrical and mechanical systems— including the installation of radiant-heat flooring—and reshaping the volumes. The second floor was originally a big open space that had a stage at one end and a piano. The third had been broken up into six rooms. We had to remove walls to transform it into an apartment with a spacious living room/sleeping loft and a separate bedroom.

To contrast the fantastic Victorian architecture, John brought in a collection of mainly 1960s and 1970s Italian furniture for the third floor, inspired by old B&B Italia ads, in which contemporary furniture had been photographed in ancient palazzos. It's very arty, with walls that are lime washed in blue and salmon, and the addition of giant speakers makes it a great location for parties. My floor is exactly the same size and layout, except that its eleven-foot-tall ceiling is three feet shorter than John's. It's tricked out with a Ping-Pong table and a basketball hoop, making it super fun for families with kids. Steve's ground-level operation, on the other hand, is very utilitarian, with restored windows and a restored shopfront.

People in the community are in love with Oddfellows Hall and what we did with it—and it has won several historic preservation awards. Better yet, as you walk down the road from the building, it's apparent that it has become an engine of urban renewal, as the houses along that stretch have started to be restored by new owners. It's had a great impact; it really changed the whole street. There didn't used to be a lot going on in Brooklin, but ever since our renovation of Odd- fellows Hall was completed, the town began to come to life again. All of my kids have told me they're quitting their jobs and moving to Brooklin with our grandchildren. I'm really optimistic about the future here.

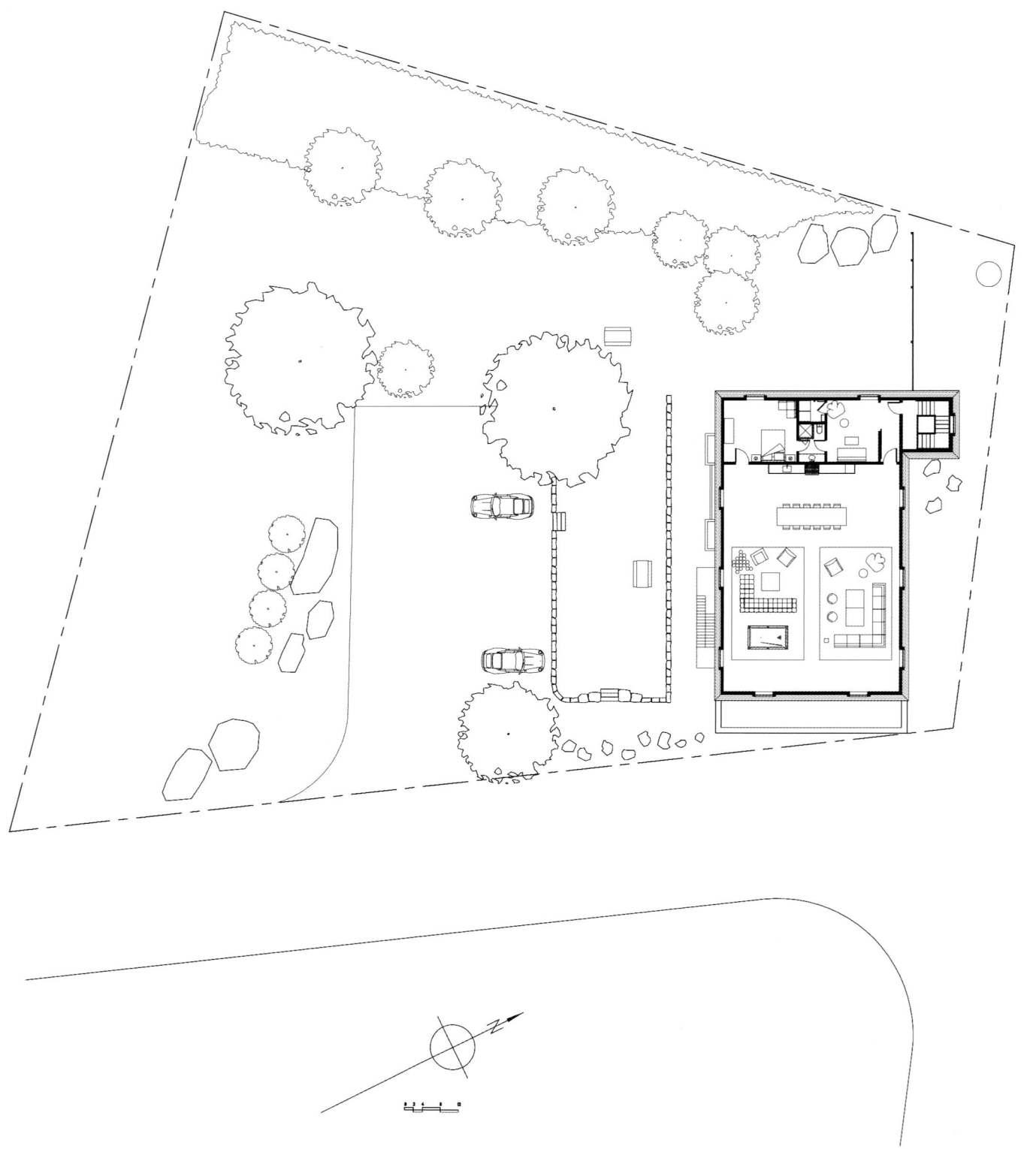

Page 117: Front door.

Page 121: East façade.

Pages 122–23: Boat shop.

Page 124: Entrance hall.

Page 125: Stair hall.

Pages 126–29: Third-floor living area.

Page 130: Site plan.

Page 131: View of Center Harbor.

Left: Bedroom.

Though John has a general idea of what he wants to achieve, there is a lot of brainstorming as a team each time IKB accepts a commission. Ultimately, our job is to figure out how to make his vision as beautiful and interesting as it can be. We all share a devotion to history and enjoy exploring architectural movements from all over the world, however obscure, and the details we research inevitably inform what we deliver to clients. We pull together disparate sources and put them in the blender—and what comes out is an IKB house.

IKB admirers with a seaside property in New York presented us with an existing house: a 1905 red-brick Georgian that was bigger than the couple required, having been designed for a way of life and a level of entertainment that doesn't really exist anymore. The living room alone could have accommodated a gala for one hundred guests. The building was also three rooms deep in most spots, which meant not only that sunlight didn't penetrate very far inside but that lots of rooms had no view of the water. Multiple parts of the house had been added over time, especially on the water side. But the clients loved the location and the varied experiences it offered. One side, the main approach, is so wooded that you think you're driving into a forest, while the other side is classic coastal New England, all water and rocks. We spent a good amount of time discussing how to renovate the house, and we drew up plans that showed what we could do if we surgically removed all the additions and revised the floor plan. Ultimately, though, it turned out that a proper renovation would cost as much as replacing the entire building. At that point the clients said, "Why don't we just build what we want?"

The answer, for them, was a classic IKB house, an Arts and Crafts design that nods to the historical style but clearly isn't a replica. For one, it is thinner and longer than the original house, basically just one room deep, so the landscape is always in view. Another departure from the Arts and Crafts norm is that the rear elevation, which faces the water, is largely glass, but the transparency is integrated in a way that feels logical even though an architect of that period would never have designed it that way. The main façade is more closed, with fewer windows, so the curtain wall comes as a surprise. Also, we didn't use any bold colors, a decision that gives the building a contemporary feeling. We settled on an austere palette that feels bleached and monochrome, with everything silvery and off-white, from the Belgian block paving to the Hispania granite to the shingles to the windows.

Within that serenity, though, are numerous potent details that seem logical and organic, too, but add elements of surprise, like the gables that thrust forward like prows, a gesture to the ocean setting. That profile is echoed indoors in the hood of the entrance hall fireplace. There is a star-shaped window that, from the exterior, looks as if the wall is being pinched open to make the shape; even the surrounding shingles are arranged to suggest that action. One of the gables has a diamond-shaped window that has the same sense of movement, except that it looks like the surface is being pried apart, the way you would separate the slats of a Venetian blind to peek out.

One of my favorite things about the house is the main staircase, which is subtle and has a lot of presence, with dark wenge spindles penetrating a banister of white oak, so you see how it was built. In typical fashion, John moseyed over to my desk one afternoon with that idea, saying it reminded him of organ pipes. It was such a John moment: coming up with an idea, dropping off the sketch, and letting me just run with it. The windows that flank the fireplace in the living room are another favorite element. That end of the room needed privacy because it faces the driveway, and the view didn't compete with that of the glass wall at the other end, but it still required something special. So I decided to use Venetian glass blocks, which let in a ton of sunlight but provide privacy because the glass is textured like water. The blocks bring to mind the small glass squares that frame the large central panes of some Victorian windows, but the pattern of the blocks—pale blue, light amber, and clear—is syncopated, like a Mondrian painting. The fireplace between the windows is made of Pewabic tiles, which were popular at the end of the nineteenth century, though they are laid in motifs that reference Eero Saarinen, the renowned mid-twentieth-century Finnish American architect. The living room's coffered ceiling recalls one at Kingscote, an 1830s Gothic Revival house in Newport that Stanford White remodeled in 1880. A door leading to the dining room is inset with a row of glass rondels— amber, blue, and clear—a detail that shows up in the work of the Italian mid-twentieth-century architect Piero Portaluppi and, coincidentally, in the front door of John's house in San Diego (see page 277).

Though there is a lot going on inside and out, the house isn't showy. It's a blend of disparate source material and unexpected combinations and ideas that, as a whole, define what an IKB house is all about: an original creation born out of a multitude of inspirations.

ROSS R. PADLUCK

Every house is unique, but the approach to preparing it to be photographed is always the same. My job—John calls me the "house whisperer"—is to bring out its soul, even if that means being ruthless. I might have to reconfigure the entire living room, but the end result is to capture what the space feels like at its best moment, in its best light, at the optimal time of day, that golden hour. It's not about reconfiguring the space to create a different room or impose a different mood. In concert with the photographer, I have to translate the visceral language of a house into the two dimensions of photography, to create the very best visual story.

At this IKB project in New York, the most important shape to my mind, the one that sets the vibe of the house, is the soaring, angular chimneypiece of folded metal in the entrance hall. Rising nearly two stories, it has a powerful presence, which meant clearing the space of any distractions that would dilute its architectural power—and then carrying that vision into every room that followed. I always identify a room's strongest, most graphic shapes and work with those to create the best composition. Little shapes usually just read as noise, even if those objects live there in real life. Harmony is the most important goal, to make the sweep of rooms feel cohesive visually.

A stylist is like a chef with a pantry full of ingredients that have to be carefully selected and combined to make the best soufflé you've ever had. I think it's also like being a line editor at a newspaper or publishing house, where you're studying a writer's words and trying to make the article or book even better and more expressive but still in the writer's voice. A lot of what I do is instinctual. On a shoot, I shift furniture, tweak how tables are positioned, edit down the accessories to reduce distractions, and bring in flowers or branches if the room needs them—and place them in exactly the right spot. Honestly, if you've ever been on a shoot, it can be like watching paint dry because the stylist is literally moving things by inches. Basically, I come in and wade through it all, identifying the strong points and the weak points to determine which arrangements of furnishings and objects really capture the feeling of the house from the viewpoint of the camera. It sounds counterintuitive, but it works.

Strangely enough, I try to make the rooms perfect but not too perfect. I don't like the standard definition of perfection, but I do work in pursuit of a level of harmony, a visual feng shui. That, to me, is very satisfying. You try to suggest to the reader that a human just passed through a space or is about to. When you walk into a house for the first time, you get a sense of its soul, and much of the time that doesn't come through in a photograph without the help of a stylist. A good stylist will enhance a room's humanity, so the camera can capture that feeling.

A house will reveal itself to you in its own time, so my first impressions of a room usually have to marinate for a day or two. My background is as a stylist and sittings editor, for editorial as well as advertising, with some thirty years of honing my eye to curate a space. Editing is something that can be undervalued or misunderstood, in part because I'm an outsider on every shoot, and my decisions might seem abrupt to the homeowner, which is why it's often better that they aren't on the premises during the shoot. The object that I'm removing from a potential shot might be one of his or her favorites, but if it doesn't work with the composition of the photograph, if it gets in the way visually, I have to get rid of it. It can always be placed somewhere else, in a better place, as the shoot progresses. The same goes for flowers, foliage, and branches that are brought into play. I look at preliminary scouting photographs, note the colors of the building, the furnishings, and the art, and keep all that in mind when I go to the flower market. Just as no one is ever sure where the camera is going to be set up in any given space, I'm never certain where the greenery is destined to go; it will end up somewhere, but again, only if it's necessary for the photograph and enhances the soul of the house. Sometimes I decide that there's no reason to photograph a particular room because it's just not important to telling the story. You can edit a house down to just a few rooms and still capture its essence.

ANITA SARSIDI

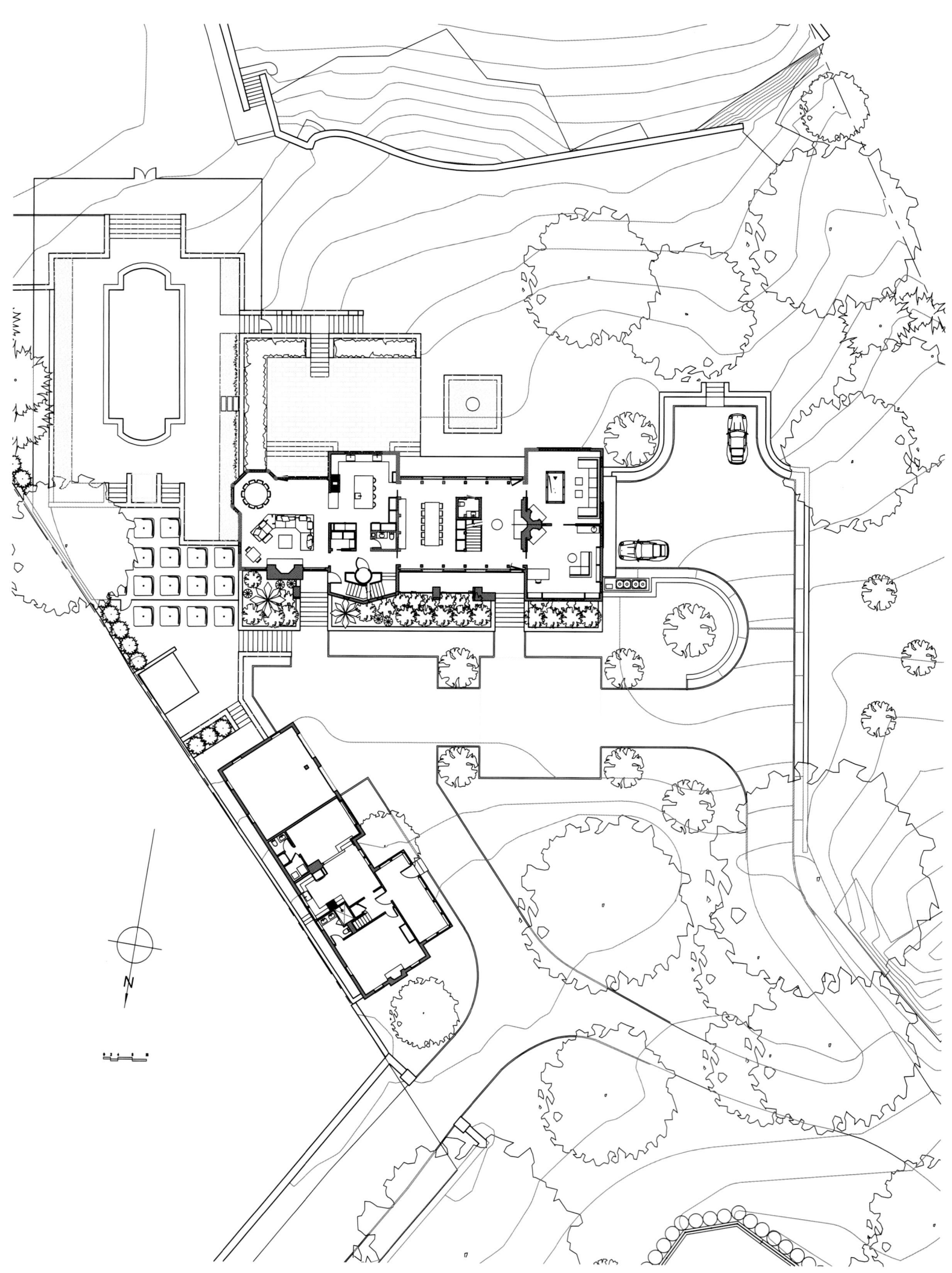

Page 135: Detail of joinery.

Pages 138–39: Northwest elevation.

Page 141: Stair tower.

Page 142: Entrance hall fireplace.

Page 143: Stair and bridge.

Page 145: Detail of balustrade.

Page 147: Second-floor hall.

Page 148: Dining room.

Page 149: Detail of door.

Pages 150–51: Family room and breakfast area.

Page 153: Family room.

Pages 154–55: Sunroom.

Page 156: Site plan.

Page 157: Elevator.

Page 158: Bedroom.

Page 159: Bathroom.

Opposite: Back porch.

Overleaf: Southeast elevation.

MOUNTAIN LODGE, CALIFORNIA | JOEL BARKLEY

Even on days when there were forty people in the office, John, Tom, and I would always seek each other out if we had an idea or a thought that needed sharing or development. We have a shared love of architecture, not just architecture in general but the byways and oddities where we often find inspiration, from traditional architecture to the proto-modern architecture of the early twentieth century. There's a hive nature to the way our brains work, and there is always the opportunity and the encouragement to take an idea and just run with it.

Often, I would see in John and Tom's work elements that I wanted to explore in my own work. Even the simplest plan John might present—say, something that appeared to be a very boxy house at first glance—would have the coolest floor plan or some other daring premise that literally took you outside the box. He's really great at the development of second-floor spaces. We all know our strengths, and there has never been any reluctance to allow someone else to have a hand in our planning.

The marching orders for this project was Adirondack Style; that's what the clients wanted. So I started researching, and in a Frank Lloyd Wright show at the Museum of Modern Art I came across some sketches that I'd never seen before. Then John went on eBay and found an old Playskool frame house and bought it for me; it proved to be an unusual but really inspiring springboard. I thought it would be a cool opportunity to design a house that was a synthesis of Wright's drawings with stone buttresses for a lodgey look, and a bit of Bernard Maybeck, all expressed within a five-sided geometry. The IKB idea is always to make something that's never been done before, a beautiful place with multiple references that says something new while also saying something old. It's a really delicate balance.

The house does have an A-frame-ish attitude but also incorporates a bit of Sir Edwin Lutyens in its 51-degree-pitched roof. One of my favorite parts of the building is the rear of the garage, where the roof slopes down to within a few feet of the ground like a blanket. In materials and sensibility, the house is also reminiscent of Bow Bay House, designed by Julia Morgan, William Randolph Hearst's court architect, in Tahoe in the 1940s. I looked at books about national parks and was really struck by the lookout towers; that led me to revisit the Mohonk Mountain House, a rugged, really romantic old hotel in New York State. All those inspirations were put into the mental blender and out came this weird, unique, delightful concoction, a sort of Shingle Style house with an Anglo accent but an all-American gutsiness. Nothing was formalized: the copper roof was left natural so it could weather, the stone was taken straight from the dig, and everything else is basically redwood shingles left to weather. Redwood houses are very moody and dramatic.

Of primary importance to the clients, whose lives are centered on family and education, was the library, which we gave pride of place at the core of the house. The clients also wanted reading nooks everywhere, so I created funny places to sit under buttresses and incorporated window seats where you can curl up with a book and get lost in the story. There's even a secret staircase that leads to the belvedere. The layout may have a storybook quality, but it is undergirded by a rigorous, formal structure, so it feels rational.

The star of the show is the roof, which is basically covered in copper squares arranged in a diagonal diamond pattern. Because it has so many different levels and variations, each section weathers in its own unique way and is as evocative as an abstract painting. The house also offers completely different views, depending on the orientation. Some take in the valley; others, the mountain. Whatever the room—primary bath, kitchen, porch—the view is dramatically different. That same sensibility is felt indoors too, where a three-sided fireplace connects the living room, dining room, and kitchen, and is also on axis with the library.

We pay a lot of attention to those relationships, the interlocking of spaces and details and how they create not only a big picture but also a multitude of little moments. There is an overall sense of balance, but if you look more closely you might see compositions and correspondences you didn't notice at first. That compositional underlay helps you begin to understand the house and its details. I take real delight in spatial relationships. It's not just about making forms, it's about creating conversations between the various aspects of the building, and the inhabitants ultimately become part of that dialogue.

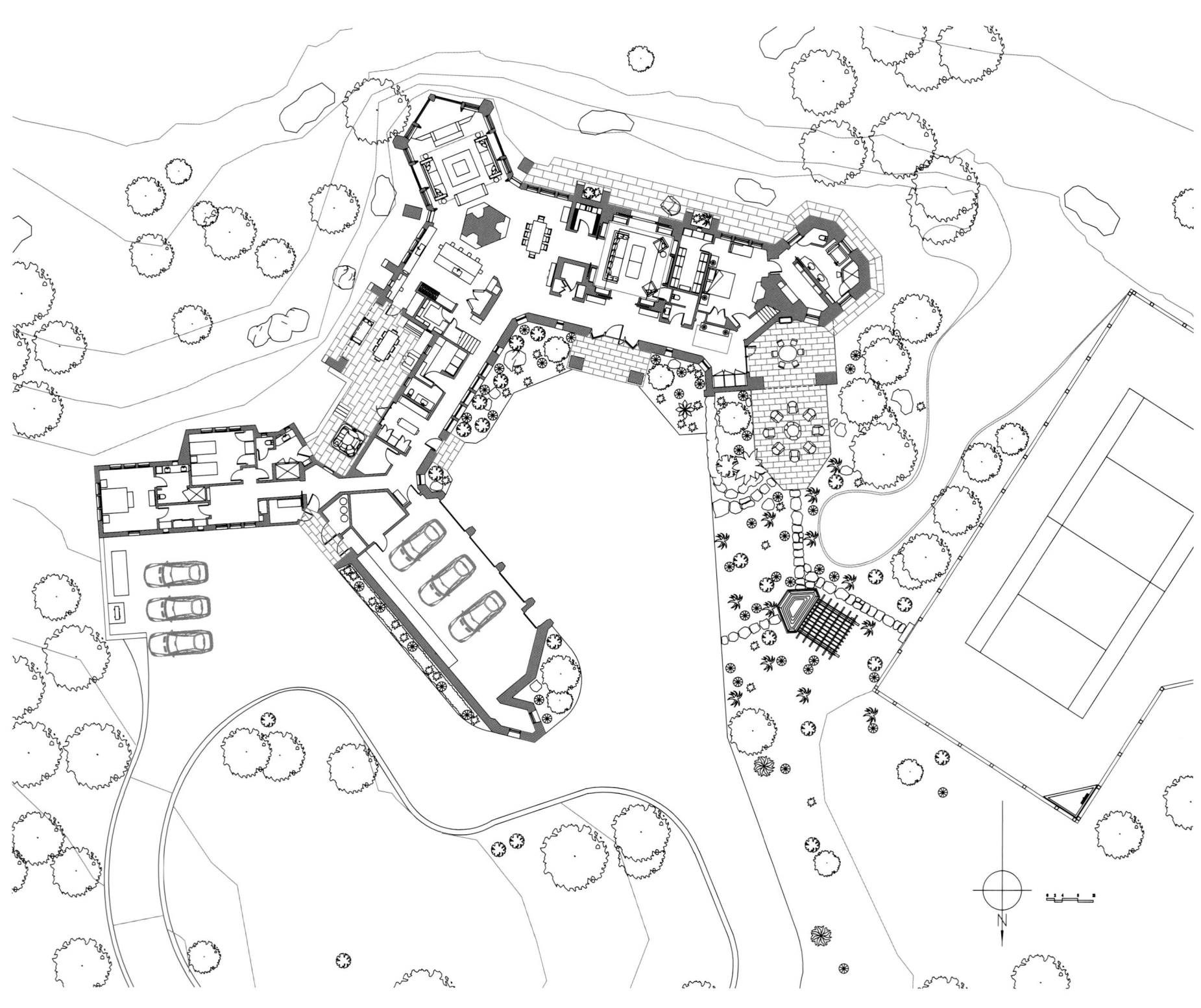

Page 165: Stone detail.

Pages 168–69: South elevation.

Pages 170–71: Aerial view.

Pages 172–73: Terrace.

Pages 174–75: Detail of dormer.

Pages 176–77: Covered porch.

Pages 178–79: Library.

Page 180: Detail of oculus.

Page 181: Library mezzanine.

Pages 182–83 left: Living room fireplace.

Pages 182–83 right: Living room.

Pages 184–85: Kitchen.

Pages 186–87: Dining room.

Pages 188–89: Bathroom.

Page 190: Site plan.

Page 191: Entrance hall.

Opposite: Detail of fireplace.

Overleaf: Tower.

A contractor has to adapt to what the architects want, which makes every job very exciting and often challenging. But you can't just take the architects' plans at their word—you must understand all the nuances and, when necessary, make the plans better. Contractors and builders have to anticipate; you don't just execute what the architect tells you. Sometimes the doors need to be thicker and heavier, or the hardware has to be heftier, and you have to be confident enough to either tell the architect that or just do it because you know it's right. Both the architectural team and my crew and I are obsessed with proportion and detail, and though there's not a lot of back and forth, we work together to achieve that.

At an IKB commission in New York—a house that is part of a complex of buildings that looks like a little village—the biggest challenge for me was the living room. It is a two-story space that runs the full width of the main building, joins the two wings, and is totally open. In addition, one side of the room features a free-standing staircase that doesn't touch any wall. Engineering the space was a feat. The plans won't tell you anything about a space like that; you have to have the experience to know how it should be constructed. You must ask yourself: How am I going to make that beautiful volume happen?

I started designing and building when I was eleven years old, in Malta, on an island called Gozo. It's an incredible place, and I absorbed a lot of design history just from growing up there. My first jobs were restoring old wooden balconies. Malta is full of houses with balconies. Nobody wanted to climb up two stories to repair them, but I wasn't afraid of heights, so I reconstructed them and repainted them. When I was twelve, I enrolled in a trade school, and by the following summer I was confident that I could build a new kitchen for my parents, using a space under my grandmother's staircase as my workshop. My parents loved the kitchen, which is still there, and my mother still uses it. Better yet, other people in Gozo liked it too. After that, I started getting calls from English residents to build bookcases and that sort of thing for their houses. I emigrated to the United States in 1979, where my brother, Mario, and I started a business in New York as cabinetmakers and general contractors. We've probably done more than 800 projects since then, including quite a few for IKB.

It's important to look at a project cohesively, as a complete entity. Everything has to be integrated: stonework, plasterwork, millwork.

No one element stands alone, and if it does, it shouldn't. John calls me a classic micromanager, and it's true. I drive my staff crazy, and some of them have been with me for more than thirty-five years. I need to know everything that's going on with all aspects of the job—and I am on call for John and his clients 24/7, including weekends. I don't want any problems. For every project, we create everything for its specific spaces and to its specific measurements in our 20,000-square-foot shop in Long Island City. We can even build full-scale models of rooms. The finished work is then transported to the building site by the crew and installed. We're very efficient, and we can build anything.

One of my favorite aspects of this project is the beamed ceiling in the living room. It's made entirely of reclaimed oak boards, and I sourced every plank by hand from an old barn that we found and dismantled. My crew pre-cut all the wood for the ceiling at the shop, and it fit perfectly in the house. We were all really excited about how beautiful it turned out and very satisfied that it went off without a hitch. Of course, I knew it would. Nobody had to cross their fingers.

John specified huge cedar brackets for the roof of the house, which has a four-foot overhang. I was worried about how the cedar brackets would hold up against the strong winds that come off the ocean. So I came up with a 3.75-inch-wide stainless-steel bracket and encased it in a cedar form. The design looks exactly like the brackets John envisioned, and though it wasn't in his plans—and I didn't tell him about it until after the brackets were in place—it works better. The brackets aren't just for looks; they really have to help anchor the roof to the house. An architect comes up with the ideas, but, as John says, a good contractor gives him and his clients another level of protection.

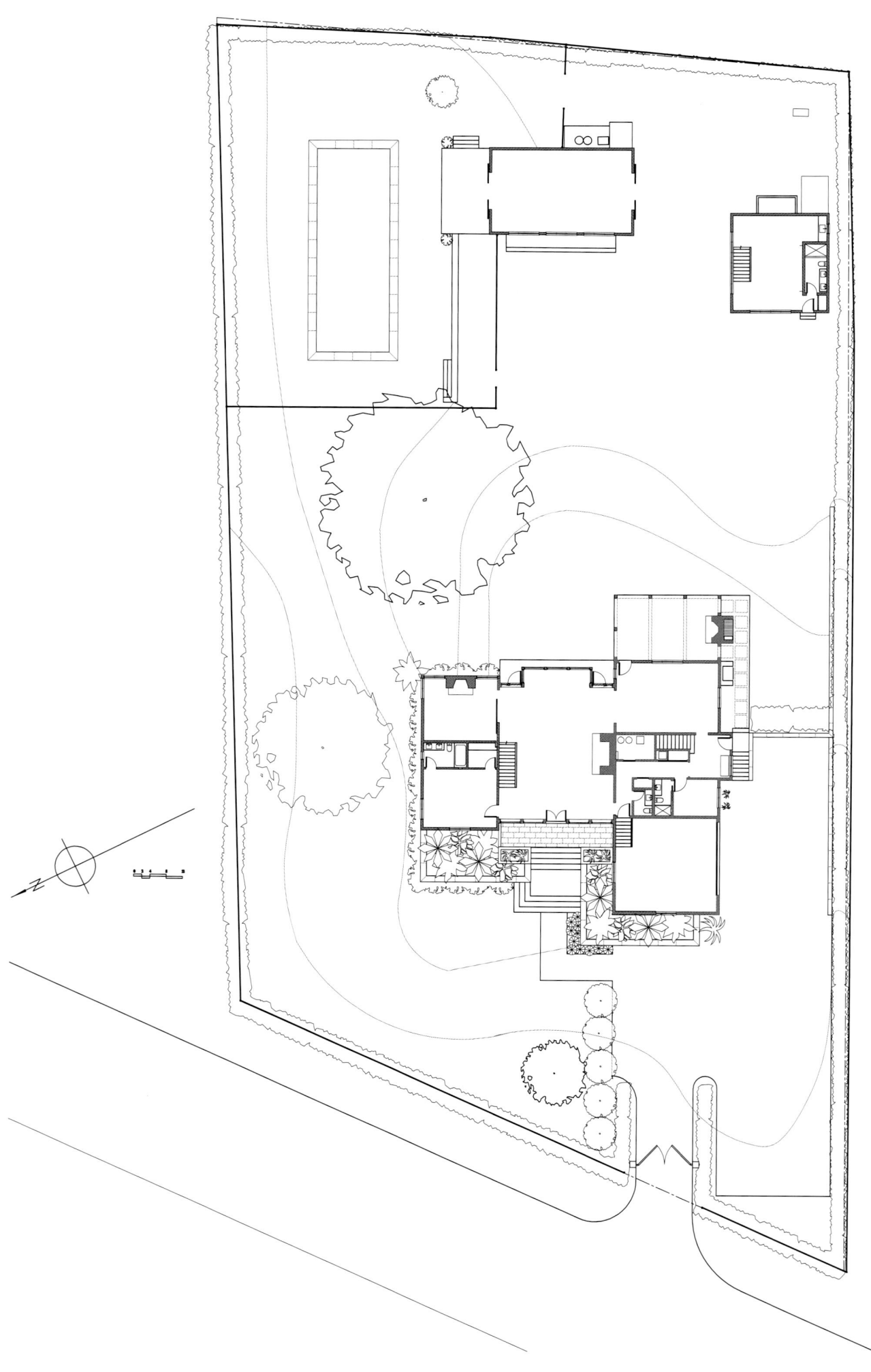

Page 197: Stairway window.

Page 201: Entry elevation.

Pages 202-3: Garden elevation.

Pages 204-5: Dining area with view of barn.

Pages 206-7: Front entrance.

Page 209: Living room.

Page 210: Stair and gallery.

Page 211: View from living room into guest room.

Page 212: View toward the dining room and kitchen.

Page 213: Kitchen.

Page 214: Bedroom.

Page 215: Bathroom.

Page 216: Site plan.

Page 217: Study with exercise bike.

Page 218: Upstairs hall.

Page 219: Bunk room.

Left: Covered porch and fireplace.

Overleaf: South elevation.

One house that I designed, a project in Sagaponack, New York, looks the way it does because of John's influence. He suggested that I might want to pull the roof down further, to make it more sheltering, more of a grounded gesture. I thought about it for a while and realized that it would make all the difference. Sometimes I see things that John does that I would do differently. He'll see something that I'm doing that isn't quite right but that I'm perhaps too close to see and will offer an observation that clarifies.

As colleagues, you absorb things every day: you overhear conversations on the phone or with teammates, you peek at drawings at the end of the day. John and I have always collaborated but not necessarily by sitting side by side. It's a forty-year partnership, a friendship. We worked together long before we started Ike Kligerman Barkley. It's a collaboration via osmosis, anchored in a combination of common insights and influences. We share a historical perspective, and we're both veterans of time well spent in the office of Robert A. M. Stern, so we solve problems in the same way. We understand each other's work in a matter of seconds, recognizing in it, whatever the style, something that we relate to because of that past.

Neither of us went whole-hog classical, though, when we went out on our own as a team. John and I both find a lot to admire in that aesthetic, but we wanted to shake up that foundation and bring contemporaneity into our work, a sense of surprise. John and I are both influenced by the architecture of the British classical mannerist Sir Edwin Lutyens, as well as by that of Austrian modernist Adolf Loos, two talents who couldn't be more different. Then again, John also admires the Italian architect Carlo Scarpa. To be honest, I must be the only architect on earth who thinks that Scarpa was a fraud. Still, John opens my eyes to people like that, often planting a seed that might—but not always—change my mind or at least broaden it.

For clients who asked for a retreat in Washington, I wanted to create an obviously contemporary house, which I don't get to do very often. The inspiration for it turned out to be a monograph that John owns about Roland Terry, a Washington State architect who had a big impact on that region's taste in the postwar era with an emphasis on streamlined silhouettes, rugged materials, and big glass windows. His buildings, such as Seattle's Canlis restaurant, are sleek but also ground hugging. I wanted to create a house that was even more open to the landscape, higher, taller, with curtain walls that opened up to the views, but that was also ensconced in a city park, so there was expansiveness and privacy at the same time. It's a friendly house, a happy house, though the palette still reflects the area: it's smoky, with fumed oak, gray tadelakt, and carbonized wood siding. The palette is limited, but thanks to the curtain walls, the building actually gleams. It lights up, inside and out, when the sun shines.

John's book about Terry sparked the project, and since he is a fan of Terry's—and I had become one—we'd casually discuss how things were going as my plans developed. Architecture is not a single-minded statement, or it shouldn't be, with apologies to Andrea Palladio and Frank Lloyd Wright. Everybody involved has a role to play in every project, to greater and lesser degrees. The clients of the Seattle house made their own impact. I had imagined that the interiors would have warmer colors; they like shades of blue, especially teal. I was slightly disappointed with that direction, but it worked out well. Every time a client wants something that I have a negative reaction to, it often turns out to be very successful. As an architect or designer, you end up working harder on things that weren't your ideas because you are forced to change your way of thinking in order to overcome your misgivings. I'm not tunnel visioned or overly proprietary like Wright. You find ways of making yourself happy when you are challenged creatively. The sauna was the client's idea too. She found it online and bought it. So we made it match the house; it looks like a miniature version of the main building, dark on the outside and luminous on the inside. It's actually pretty wonderful and adds a great deal, visually and experientially.

The major lesson I've learned from working with John is not to worry quite so much, not to overthink details to the point where you believe that the detail is all that matters. He's honestly loosened me up over the years. You want your projects to be resolved, but you also have to be sensitive to the vagaries of the human mind, the eye of the beholder. Sometimes the architect might think something could be better, should be better, but if the composition is good and there's a strong idea driving the whole concept, then it's good. Perfection is the one thing that John has taught me to steer clear of—most of the time.

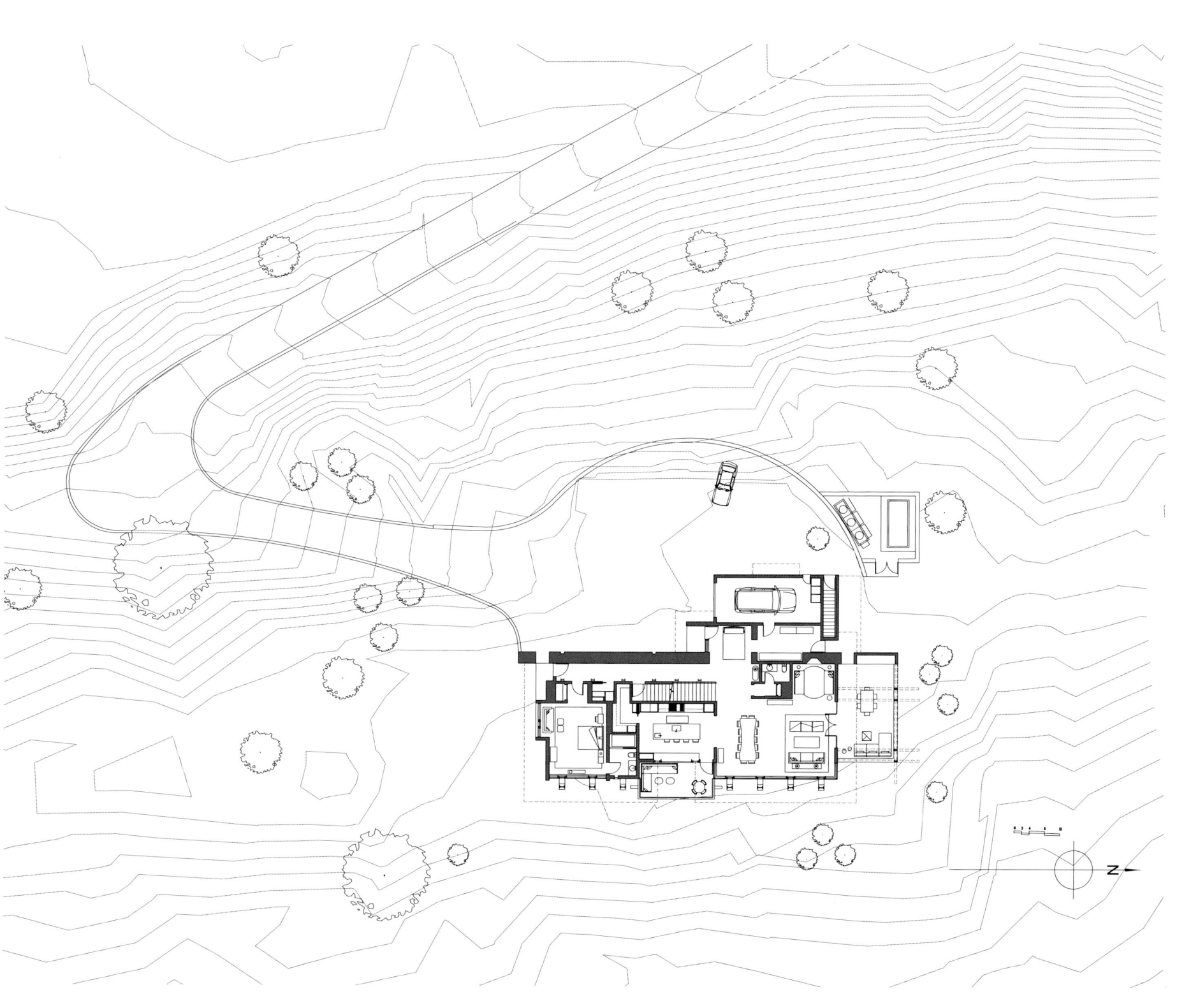

Page 225: Detail of balcony.

Pages 228–29: East elevation.

Page 230: Front entrance.

Page 231: Detail of colonnade.

Pages 232–33: Entry court.

Pages 235–36: Living room.

Page 237: Inglenook.

Page 238: Stair hall.

Page 239: Dining area.

Pages 240–41: Bunk room.

Page 242: Site plan.

Page 243: South elevation.

Opposite: Sauna.

VINEYARD ESTATE, CALIFORNIA | CARL BAKER

Much of IKB's California work is remodels. Believe it or not, there's a dearth of buildable land in a state this big, so people frequently purchase a house that isn't perfect and then turn to our San Francisco office for ways to improve it. I love helping an existing house. It's all about embracing the constraints and drawbacks and turning them to your advantage. Challenges make you work harder to find solutions.

A couple came to us after purchasing a 1970s ranch house in a Napa Valley neighborhood literally built within vineyards. The vines come up to the property lines, sometimes to the houses themselves, as you see at wine châteaux in France. The first problem that we needed to solve was the public exposure—the couple's house was fully visible to all passersby and reached by a straight path from the street to a big front porch with stout stucco columns. Though the porch overlooked acres of grapevines and nothing else, it felt pretentious. All of us—the IKB team and the clients—felt that the building needed to disappear from view and that the property had to be reimagined in favor of mystery, charm, and, most of all, privacy. That goal got the conversation going: how to make the house feel like it was in the middle of the countryside rather than in a development, flanked by other houses, however nice that development might be—effortless and understated but at the same time layered and rich.

We decided to remove the walk and extend an existing boxwood hedge almost all the way across the front of the property to obscure the street but not the view of the vineyard opposite. Then we shifted the entrance to a back corner of the house, tucked into the property and adjacent to the driveway. That move really changed the character of the building and how you experience it: a humble entrance that you have to search for, rather than an axial va-va-voom that's right in your face. Now you reach the front door via a stone walkway that meanders through plantings of roses, lavender, and olive trees, a sun-dappled approach that was created by landscape designer Elaine Shaw. She also turned the front yard into a meadow of wildflowers and grasses, so the house feels nestled in the countryside. That's the view that the glass-walled breakfast room—the former front porch—looks onto: meadow in front, with a smattering of olive trees, the boxwood hedge in the middle, and the grapevines and sky beyond.

Ultimately, we changed almost everything while largely working within the existing footprint. Beams were beefed up here and boxed in there

to create a peaceful internal rhythm that isn't necessarily noticed but that you can certainly feel. Detailing is simple and limited, with a nod toward both Japanese and Western traditions, again in pursuit of a sense of calmness and coherence. We selected the materials in the same way, especially the introduction of walnut, a warm yet sophisticated wood that shows up throughout the house, from windows to doors and lintels to casework.

The openwork screen that divides the entrance hall and the kitchen is also made of walnut; we felt that it was important for the kitchen to feel transparent rather than sealed off, as it often is, and, unlike a standard wall, the screen invites light and air to circulate while ensuring that anybody in the kitchen is a part of the action. In addition, the screen allows you to see visitors arriving, an experience that feels very countrified to me. When visitors enter the house and walk past the screen, they end up in the living room, where they can see the rear garden at one end and the breakfast porch and meadow at the other. The sequencing of the spaces was really fun to develop.

Some of the axis points were realigned too: we centered the gable in the kitchen and emphasized or created centerlines for light fixtures. Yet, our team didn't feel it was necessary to fix every irregularity that we encountered. A case in point is the fireplace in the former living room. After we divided that open space into a family area and the dining area, the fireplace was off-center, but we ended up loving it. It became one of those moments where architectural symmetry is broken in a nice way, a sweet little idiosyncrasy. It is now topped by a sculpted maple mantel.

The living room is a new addition, a double-height space that breaks the low-slung ranch house volume. Located on the opposite side of the house from the breakfast room, it juts into the garden and overlooks the swimming pool, which is surrounded by a simple farm fence that is covered with white-flowering jasmine. We moved an existing pergola to one side of the living room to create a shaded outdoor dining area.

We also reorganized the primary bedroom and bathroom wing, rejiggering the layout so we could insert an office nook in the corridor and adding more windows for maximal natural light. Wherever you are in the house, you're always aware of the gardens, the sunlight, and the breezes.

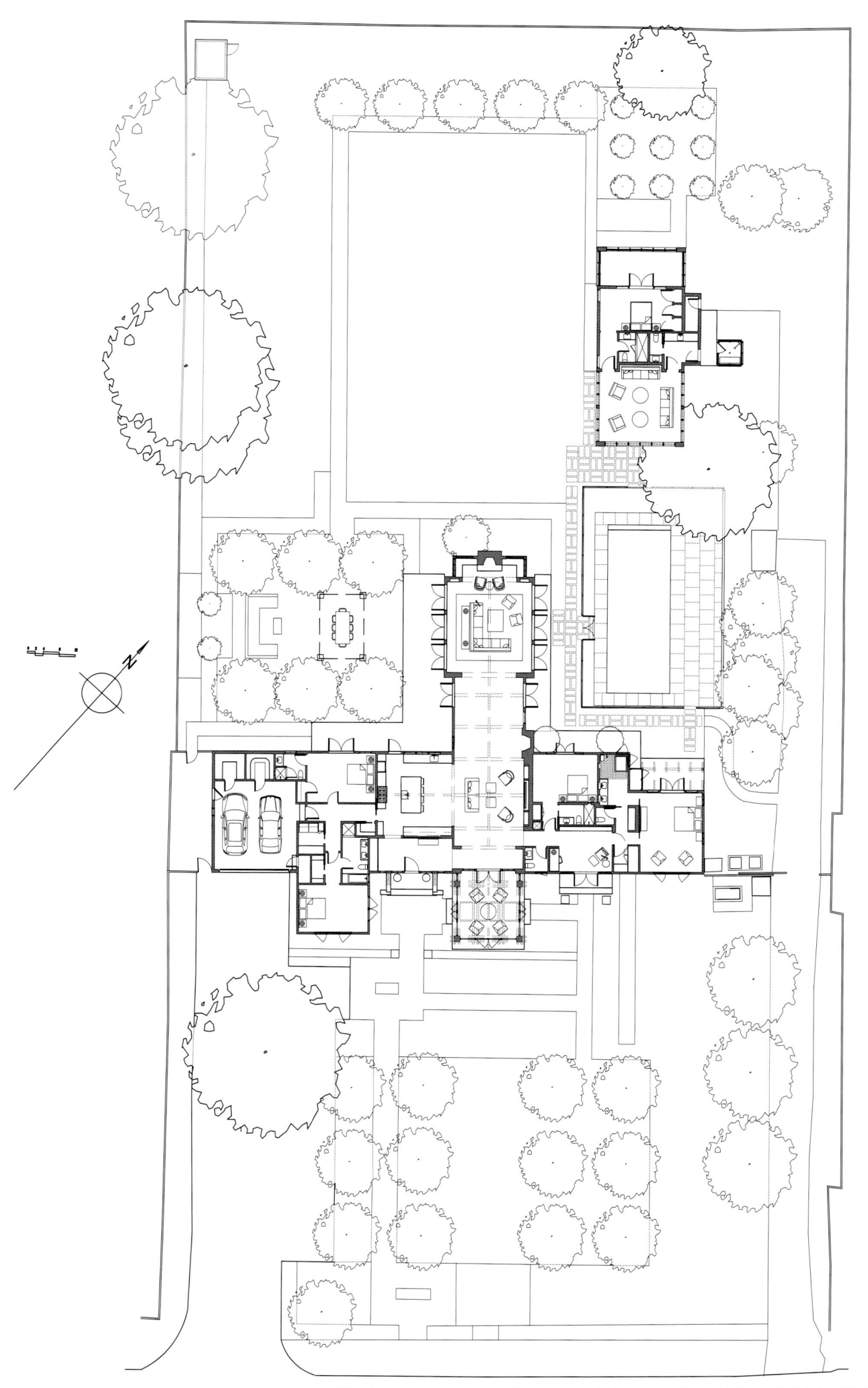

Page 247: View of vineyard.

Pages 250–51: Entrance garden.

Pages 252–53: Dining porch.

Pages 254–55: Living room.

Pages 256–57: Dining area.

Page 258: Entrance hall.

Page 259: Site plan.

Left: Kitchen.

Overleaf: Pool house.

Pages 264–65: Vineyard.

CASITA, CALIFORNIA | JUDY KAMEON

When I was a painter, my work was about patterns, color, scale, varying silhouettes, transparency, and opacity. Transitioning into landscape design was quite natural, though it offered me a much richer palette, a different sense of scale, and silhouettes in three dimensions, as well as fragrances and sounds and textures. Paintings are inert, but gardens are immersive; they change and evolve.

For John's house in San Diego, which backs onto a steep slope, his marching orders were simple. He loves the way the hillsides in Ravello, an Italian coastal town, are terraced with citrus groves that descend to the sea. He also likes how I landscaped my own property, which includes a ravine. Basically, that's about all he told me, giving me a very free hand. The front of his property is level, although the house, a 1940s modernist bungalow, is set back just far enough from the street that there was sufficient space to accomplish what I like to do best: devise a multilayered garden that inspires engagement, carving out spaces that invite cooking, entertaining, having a nap, or reading a book. A landscape with multiple purposes intrigues me: What is a front yard supposed to be? One thing it shouldn't be anymore is the old model of a lawn with a lollipop tree and a border of flowers. Monoculture makes for a weak infrastructure, which means if one part fails, everything fails.

A garden should look inviting even when nothing is in bloom. At John's house, I relied on Mediterranean and subtropical plants with sculptural qualities and lively textures: cacti, euphorbia, thyme, sedums, agaves, aloes. One of the anchors is an organ cactus, which has grown into a giant green sculpture straight out of a Dr. Seuss illustration. Another is an existing plumeria tree, which behaves totally differently in Southern California than it does in its native Hawaii. Here, it usually doesn't produce many leaves but has spectacular blossoms and an amazing branch structure, which more than makes up for the lack of conventional greenery. The plumeria is one example of how I like to preserve existing elements of a landscape, so the property maintains a connection to its past. Even if that means relocating those original plants—as I did with John's roses, which had been planted by a previous owner—to better locations. There's really no reason to start over completely. Varieties that attract birds and butterflies are important, too, which means that there has to be a diversity of plant materials and a succession of flowers and fragrances. The result is a tapestry of plants that are knitted together for year-round enjoyment.

That layering begins in the public space, namely the sidewalk, and crosses over into the private space. Procession is something we think about a lot in our office: how to enhance the experience—or more clearly, experiences—that you get as you walk from the street to the front door. It should never be a straight shot. The front door might be visible, but there should be a bit of mystery as to how to arrive at it. It should be off in the distance, separated from you by layers of plant material of different sizes and colors and textures. By the time you open the front gate at John's house and make your way to the entrance porch, you have already had multiple experiences: visual, spatial, and sensory.

Your eye should be diverted, too, by a water feature here, a raised planter there, a fire pit, even a dining terrace off the kitchen, all of which we worked into John's front yard. We enclosed the yard with a waist-high wall of concrete blocks, which spoke to the mid-century moment when John's house was built, as well as to the stacked walls that are associated with the work of Southern California architect A. Quincy Jones. The wall provided a new sense of structure and gave us the chance to incorporate built-in seating. That was yet another nod to postwar architecture, when built-in furnishings were so common inside a house. At John's, though, the built-ins are outside. There's a masonry ledge on the dining terrace that is softened with cushions, creating an invitation to come outside, to lounge and hang out. It really is one large open-air destination for dining, drinks, or conversation, balancing the cantilevered wood terrace that John added to the other side of the building. So much of the pleasure of John's house is how it extends into the landscape and melds with it.

That being said, if an exterior area doesn't feel private, people won't use it—and private doesn't have to mean literally hidden from view. From the front terrace at John's house, you can see the surrounding houses and get glimpses of the street and traffic, too, yet the way it has been framed—with the wall, trees, and plants—you feel secure and protected.

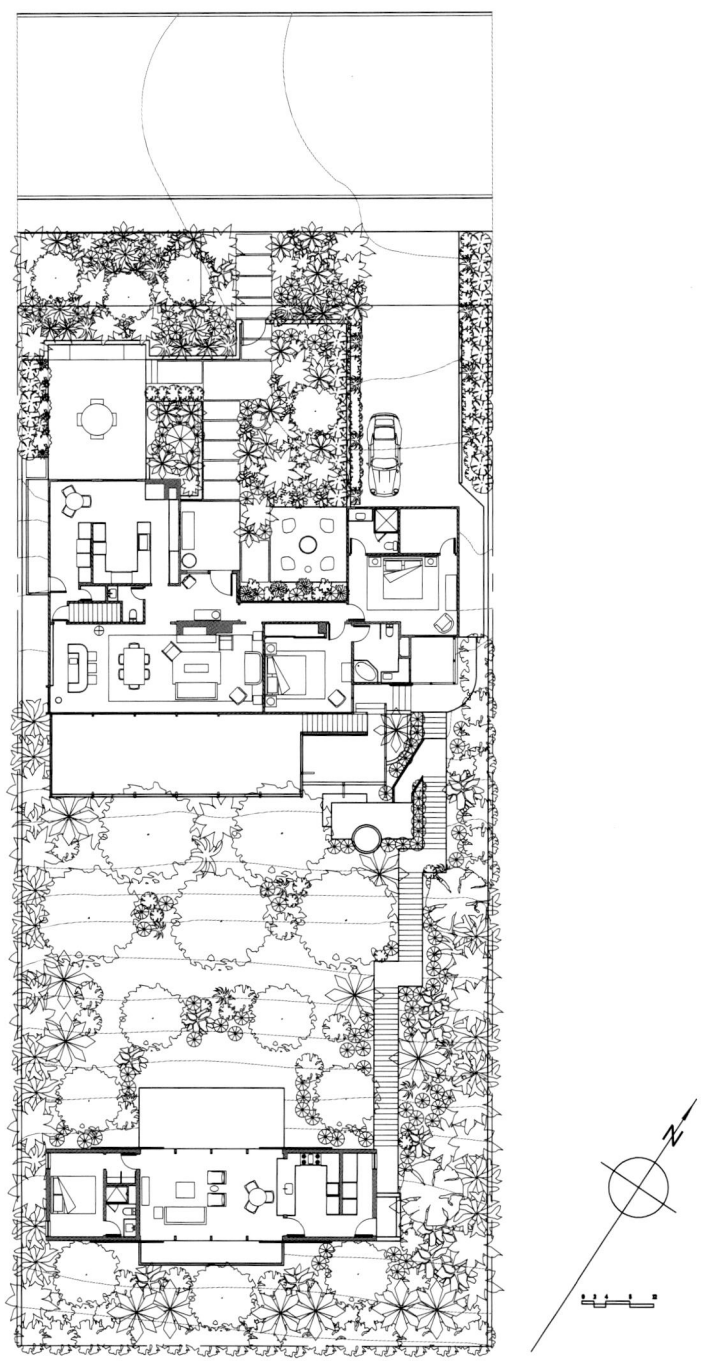

Page 267: Detail of living room.

Pages 270–71: View from street.

Page 272: Agave.

Page 273: Aerial view of entrance garden.

Pages 274–75: West elevation.

Page 277: Entrance hall.

Pages 278–79: Living room.

Page 280: Detail of wall hanging.

Page 281: Dining area.

Page 283: Bar.

Page 285: Detail of bedroom.

Pages 286–87: Bedroom.

Page 289: Bathroom.

Pages 290–91: Guesthouse bedroom.

Pages 292–93: Guesthouse living room.

Page 294: Site plan.

Page 295: Hot tub.

Pages 296–97: Guesthouse.

Opposite: Guesthouse and main residence.

ACKNOWLEDGMENTS

This book, at its core, is an acknowledgement of all those who've worked together to realize these projects. There are hundreds, if not thousands, of people who have contributed in a variety of ways to the houses in the book. The few who have told their stories within represent but the tip of the iceberg.

Our clients, without whom none of this would be possible, have been trusting, patient, and enthusiastic beyond measure.

I owe a debt of gratitude to our incredible team of architects, interior designers, and staff throughout the years. My Ike Kligerman Barkley partners, Tom Kligerman and Joel Barkley, and my colleagues Ross Padluck and Mia Jung, have been inspirational and supportive through thick and thin.

My new Ike Baker Velten partners, Carl Baker and Tyler Velten, and staff are courageous and trusting as we embark on our new venture and hope to create the next chapter in this evolving tale.

My thanks to the many consultants, colleagues, and collaborators, including interior designers, landscape architects, builders, crafts-people, and artists, who enliven and enrich each of these projects.

Mark Magowan and Jacqueline Decter and the entire Vendome team have been enthusiastic and supportive and made this entire process a joy. Cynthia Conigliaro, a longtime friend, was instrumental in get-ting this book pointed in the right direction. Photographers Richard Powers, William Waldron, Roger Davies, and Nicole Franzen have beautifully captured both the architecture and the ambience of each project. Mary Shanahan, Mitch Owens, Sara Frantz, Anita Sarsidi, and I met almost a year ago in the living room of my San Diego house and laid down a very solid foundation for this book. It has contin-ued to be fun and fulfilling throughout the process. And thank you, Molly Denver, for the beautiful drawings and all the help throughout the years.

Finally, I'd like to thank my family—Kathy, Andy, Emily, Sally, and Gritty—and all my friends for their love and encouragement.

CREDITS

RANCH HOUSE, California
Architect: John Ike with Tyler Velten and Molly Denver
Builder: Vucina Construction, Inc.
Landscape: Nature with the help of the owner and Tyler Velten
Furniture and Décor: John Ike
Photography: Richard Powers with Anita Sarsidi

SEASIDE VILLA, New Jersey
Architect: John Ike with Ross Padluck and Jen Huang
Builder: Vincent Sollecito
Landscape: Enea Garden Design New York / Enea Jaimes
Landscape Architecture DPC
Furniture and Décor: John Ike with Mia Jung and Kaycee Park
Lighting: Orsman Design, Inc.
Photography: Richard Powers with Anita Sarsidi

ODDFELLOWS HALL, Maine
Architect: John Ike with Molly Denver
Builder: Robert A. Baird & Associates
Landscape: Robert A. Baird
Furniture and Décor: John Ike
Photography: Richard Powers with Anita Sarsidi

MODERN SHINGLISH, New York
Architect: John Ike with Ross Padluck and Michael Stonikinis
Builder: Hobbs, Inc.
Landscape: Janice Parker Landscape Architects
Furniture and Décor: Stacey Gendelman Designs
Photography: Richard Powers with Anita Sarsidi

MOUNTAIN LODGE, California
Architect: Joel Barkley with Carl Baker and Ken Avery
Builder: Jones Corda Construction
Furniture and Décor: The Wiseman Group
Photography: Roger Davies (pages 168-69, 176-89, 191, 192) and
Richard Powers (pages 165, 170-75, 194-95)

CONTEMPORARY CRAFTSMAN, New York
Architect: John Ike with Ross Padluck
Builder: Frank M. DeBono Construction Corporation
Landscape: Ross Padluck with Marders Landscaping
Furniture and Décor: Owner
Photography: Richard Powers with Anita Sarsidi

GLASS HOUSE, Washington
Architect: Thomas A. Kligerman with Joe Carline
Builder: Jim Dow, Dowbuilt
Landscape: Dodi Fredericks, Fredericks Landscape Architecture
Furniture and Décor: Mia Jung with Elizabeth Sesser
and Patricia Cassidy
Photography: Richard Powers with Anita Sarsidi

VINEYARD ESTATE, California
Architect: Carl Baker with Tyler Velten and Georgy Avakov
Builder: Jim Murphy & Associates
Landscape: Elaine Shaw Landscape Architecture
Furniture and Décor: Dan Fink Studio
Photography: Nicole Franzen (pages 256-58) and
Roger Davies (pages 247, 250-55, 260-65)

CASITA, California
Architect: John Ike with Ross Padluck
Builders: Mcguiness Construction, Inc., and Sean Tobacco
Landscape: Judy Kameon, Elysian Landscapes
Furniture and Décor: John Ike
Photography: Richard Powers (pages 270-75, 277, 280-81, 285-87,
290-93, 295-97, 299) and William Waldron (pages 267, 278-79, 283,
289) with Anita Sarsidi

John Ike: 9 Houses, 9 Stories
First published in 2023 by The Vendome Press
Vendome is a registered trademark of The Vendome Press LLC

VENDOME PRESS US
P.O. Box 566
Palm Beach, FL 33480

VENDOME PRESS UK
Worlds End Studio
132-134 Lots Road
London, SW10 0RJ

www.vendomepress.com

Distributed in North America by Abrams Books
Distributed in the United Kingdom, and the rest of the world, by
Thames & Hudson

ISBN 978-0-86565-427-3

Publishers: Beatrice Vincenzini, Mark Magowan,
and Francesco Venturi
Editor: Jacqueline Decter
Production Director: Jim Spivey
Designer: Mary Shanahan

Library of Congress Cataloging-in-Publication Data
available upon request

Printed and bound in China by
RR Donnelley (Guangdong) Printing Solutions
Company Ltd

Page 1: California live oak.

Pages 2-3: Aerial view of Ranch House.

Pages 4-5: Seaside Villa.

Pages 6-7: Casita.

Page 8: Detail of patinated-copper shingle roof,
Mountain Lodge.

Page 11: Detail of terrazzo floor, Seaside Villa.

Page 12: Entrance hall fireplace, Modern Shinglish.

Pages 300, 303: Details of window, Modern Shinglish.

Page 301: John Ike.

First printing

All of these photographs are by Richard Powers.